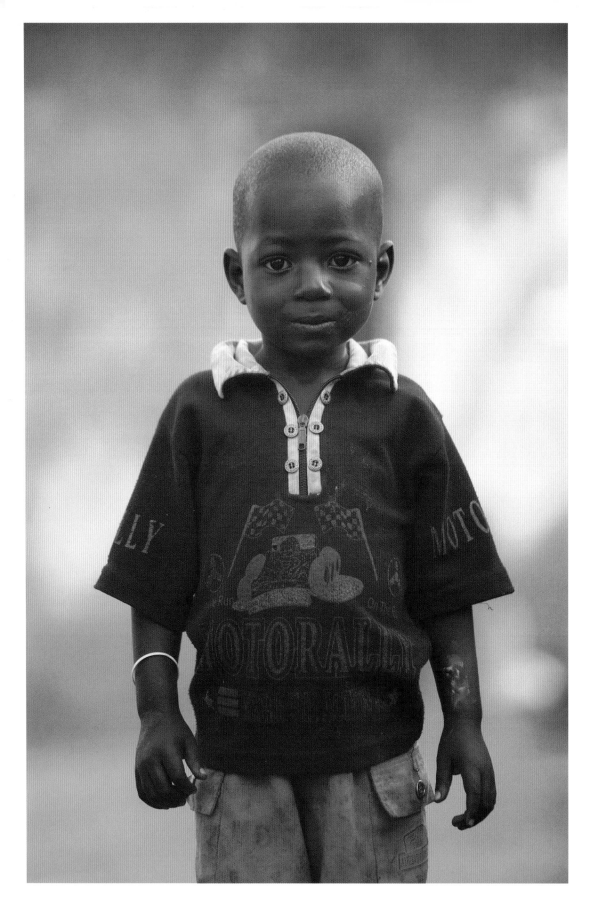

DESPAIR

HOPE

WATOTO

WATOTO

IN THE SWAHILI LANGUAGE OF EAST AFRICA, WATOTO MEANS 'THE CHILDREN'.

TO THE DESTITUTE CHILDREN OF UGANDA, WATOTO MEANS 'HOPE'.

Humble beginnings. In 1994 Gary and Marilyn Skinner established Watoto Child Care Ministries [www.watoto.com] as a compassionate response to the orphan crisis confronting the East African Nation of Uganda. With approximately 2 million children in Uganda, orphaned through the scourge of civil war and the AIDS epidemic, the situation is both very real and very urgent.

Watoto is a holistic childcare program targeted towards meeting the essential needs of parentless children. Watoto's goal is to provide spiritual, physical, educational and emotional care for every child so that each one will become a responsible Christian and productive citizen of Uganda. With a vision to reach tens of thousands of children, Watoto is committed to raising the next generation of Ugandan leaders.

Strategy. Watoto cares for children in two ways. Single-family dwellings are constructed to provide shelter for the most destitute children. Watoto is strongly committed to placing the children in a family environment rather than in large institutional orphanages. Watoto accepts children between the ages of 2 and 12 and once in Watoto the children remain a part of their new family for life. Eight children and a 'house mother' live in one of the homes that volunteer teams from around the world fund and construct. The homes consist of three bedrooms, a kitchen, living area and bathroom with clean running water and power. Watoto

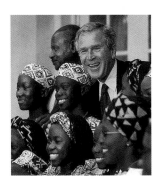

Children's Villages include clusters of these homes, a primary school, high school, water project, medical clinic and a multi-purpose hall for use as a church and community centre. Watoto also assists relatives to care for parentless children in their extended families by providing education, clothing and food.

The strategy is based on the belief that as the children are trained academically and spiritually, they will enter society equipped with the necessary life skills and moral values enabling them to make a significant and lasting impact on the future of Uganda and the African continent.

Watoto Children's Choir. Since 1994 Watoto Children's Choirs have toured internationally as ambassadors for Watoto Child Care Ministries. The 'Concerts of Hope' inform people of Watoto's life-saving nation-changing work and afford people the opportunity to participate in restoring hope and dignity to some of Africa's most needy children. The Choir consists of 18 boys and girls who have endured the agony of losing one or both of their parents and who now live in Watoto homes. Accompanying the children is a group of adults from Uganda who supervise and care for the children while touring.

Together the Choir presents Watoto's vision through their music and dance, which is an energetic fusion of contemporary gospel and traditional African rhythm. 'Concerts of Hope' are a lively demonstration of the life-changing love of God experienced by the children of Watoto. Audiences across the globe have been deeply moved by the life saving message of hope that Watoto's children bring.

Today Watoto is impacting the lives of thousands of orphans by providing physical, emotional, educational and spiritual care to some of Uganda's most vulnerable children. The vision of caring for tens of thousands of Uganda's orphans remains strong.

Uganda's children DESPERATE,
Two million orphans due to HIV AIDS and war;
the highest number per capita in the world.

Conditions unimaginable

Hopelessness unbearable

Pain insufferable

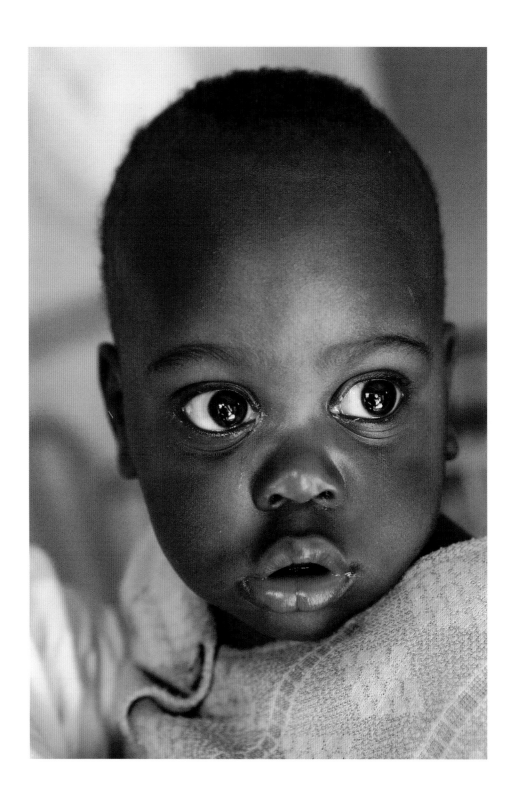

Moments of joy so rare

When no one cares.

"We worry about what a child will becom

omorrow, yet we forget
that he is someone today."

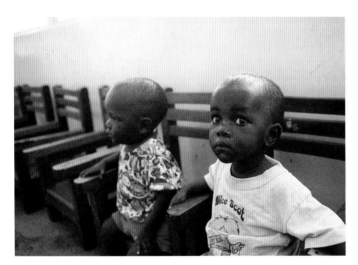

Children abandoned and institutionalised,

thrown on the garbage heaps and pit latrines of life.

"Children are the living message we send to a tim

e will not see."

John W. Whitehead, The Stealing of America, 1983

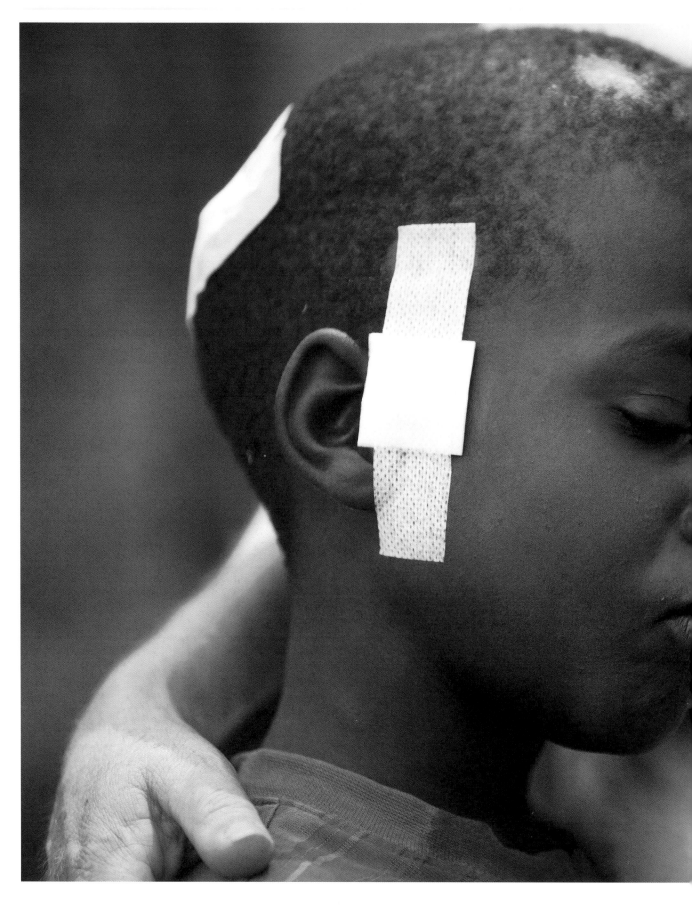

"For I know the plans I have for you,"
declares the Lord, "plans to prosper you
and not to harm you, plans to give you
HOPE and a future."

JEREMIAH 29:11

The Journey towards HOPE is long and hard.
It is never taken alone, we are all RESPONSIBLE.

Works, not Words,

are the proof of love.

If there is anything better than

being loved,

it is loving.

"A mother is the truest friend we have,
when trials heavy and sudden, fall upon us; when adversity takes the place of
prosperity; when friends who rejoice with us in our sunshine desert us;
when trouble thickens around us, still will she cling to us, and endeavour by her kind
precepts and counsels to dissipate the clouds of darkness,
and cause peace to return to our hearts."

Washington Irving

UGANDA

Uganda is a member of the British Commonwealth and gained its independence in 1962. With a population of over 26 million people it has a literacy rate of only 52%. The official language is English although Swahili and other dialects abound in tribal regions.

Most notoriously, the country is remembered for its dictator Idi Amin, deposed in 1979. His rule of terror commenced in January 1971 when the ruling President, then Milton Obote, was out of the country attending a Commonwealth Heads of State Conference in Singapore. Amin staged a coup of the government offices and quickly took over as President. Britain was one of the countries that recognised the new regime but little did they realise what a future they had endorsed for this nation. Later that year, the Israeli 'Raid on Entebbe' caused a major embarrassment to Amin but it did nothing to stop his eight year rule of terror. Amin's death squads slaughtered more than 300,000 people during the period from 1971 to 1979. The nationalisation of its industries and the eventual pilfering of its assets by Amin and his cronies brought the once prosperous country to financial ruin. Looters and poachers, leaving behind only a few species of what was once an abundance of African wildlife, decimated natural game parks. Driven out of Uganda in 1979, Amin found exile in Jeddah whilst Milton Obote took over the reigns of the country and another 300,000 Ugandans were mercilessly slaughtered under his reign.

The National Resistance Army led by Yoweri Museveni began to grow a few months after Obote took over power. With a nucleus of just 27 men it grew to a force of over 20,000 instilled with the ideology of being servants of the people, not their oppressors. Following a civil war in 1986, Museveni was installed as President of Uganda.

Today a new evil threatens Uganda in the shape of HIV AIDS. It is carving destruction through the African continent with estimates of over 15 million children having been orphaned. The largest number of AIDS orphans per capita anywhere in the world is in Uganda where it is conservatively estimated that there are 2 million orphans, just under 10% of the population. This is nothing short of a catastrophe.

Yet the Ugandan Church has not forgotten its people. Through the Church's love and generosity there is hope. Through the vision of organisations like Watoto the parentless generation is finding love, security and value. Truly the next generation of Ugandan leaders will be found through such as Watoto.

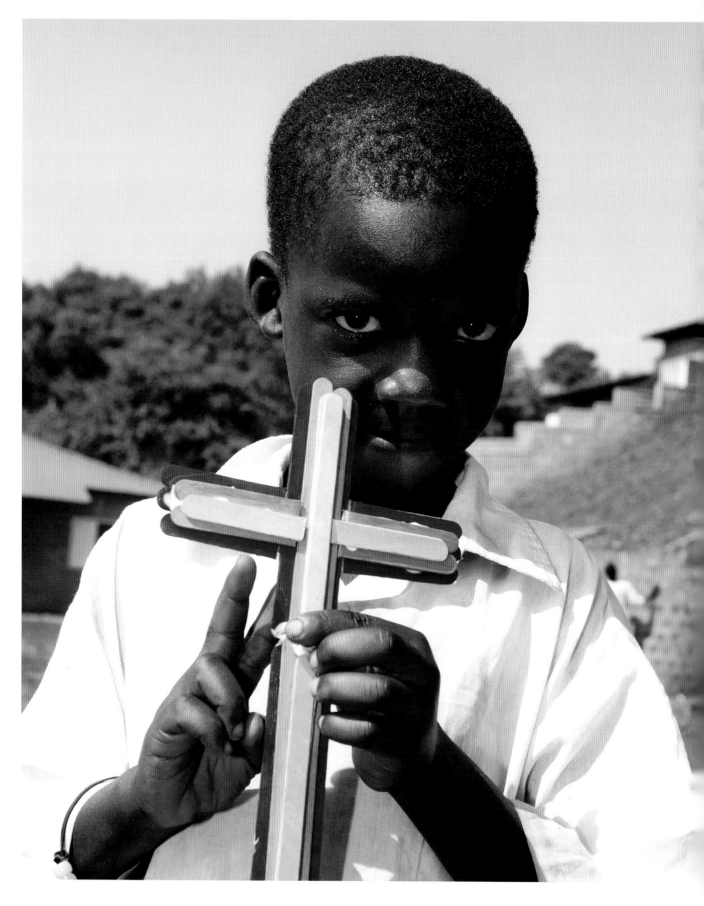

Faith gives us the courage to face today with

confidence

and tomorrow with
expectancy.

Hope is the anchor of the Soul, the stimulus to action

he **momentum** to achieve great things.

Where there is hope, there is belonging.

"Those who hope in the Lord will renew their strength.
They will soar on wings likes eagles;
they will run and not grow weary;
they will walk and not be faint."

ISAIAH 40:31

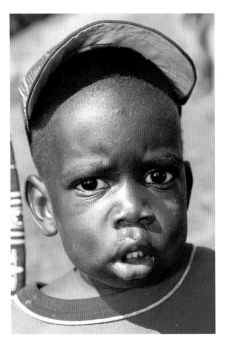  

"Hope is its strongest when the future is before you."

Pastor Steve Peach

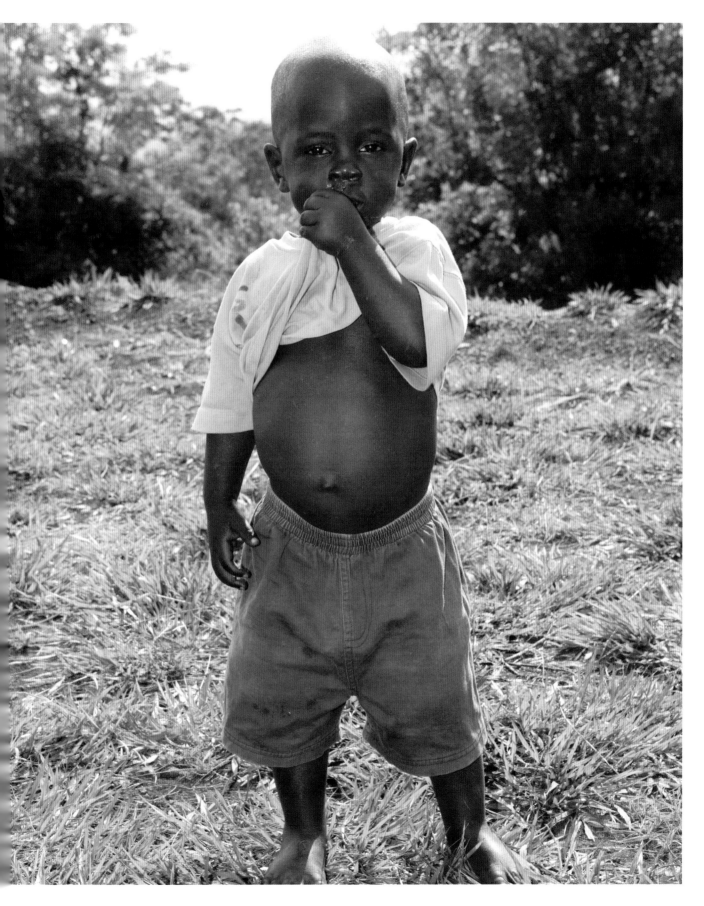

"Good family life
is never an accident, but an achievement by
those who share it."

James H. Bossard

WATOTO's vision is to raise the next
generation of Uganda's leaders.

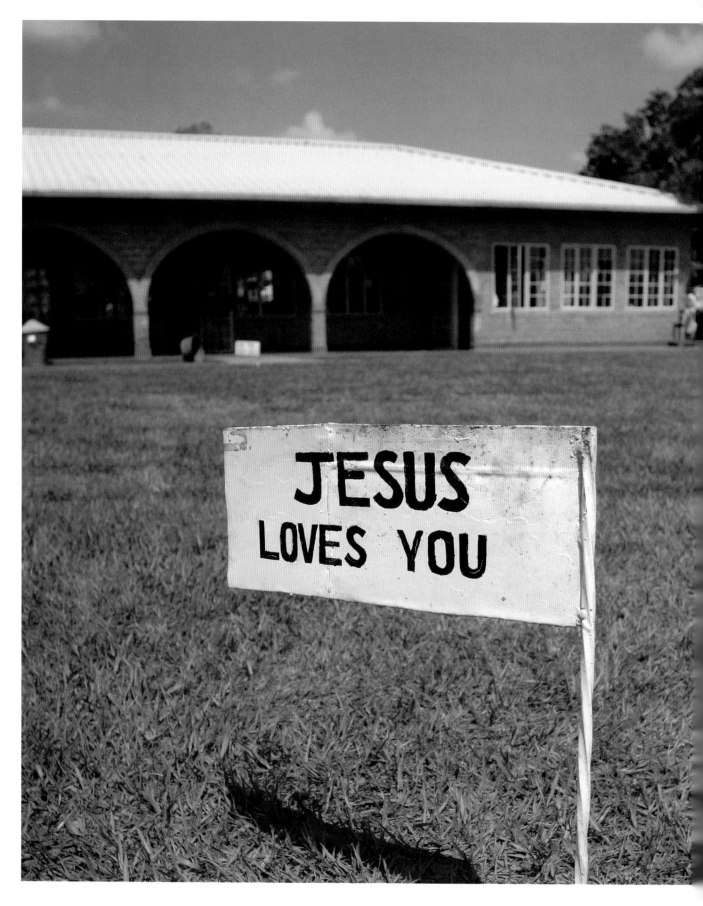

Life is the time God gives us to decide where
we want to spend

eternity.

"There are no seven wonders of the world
in the eyes of a child. There are seven million."

Walt Streightiff

" Children are one third of our populatio

...nd all of our future."

Select Panel for the Promotion of Child Health, 1981

The HOPE of Watoto is **founded** in providing the physical, spritual, educational and emotional care for every child so that each one will become a responsible Christian and productive citizen of Uganda.

"Train a child in the way he should go and

when he is old he **will not** turn from it."

It takes a village to raise a child.

Ancient African Proverb

"Hope deferred makes the heart sick, bu

a longing fulfilled is a tree of life."

PROVERBS 13:12

Watoto takes despair

and turns it into HOPE.

The Journey has just Begun

The Watoto vision to address the need of the parentless child is unique. With a non-institutional focus on caring for orphaned children in a home with a house mother, Watoto focuses on the individual within the community. With an initial vision to care for 10,000 orphaned children, Watoto is committed to raising the next generation of Ugandan leaders.

If this journey has touched your heart, remember it is only the beginning. Only through people partnering with Watoto can the first step of caring for 10,000 of the neediest children on the planet be realised. Your support has an immediate and lasting impact, taking children from crushing poverty and despair into hope. More information on how you can support this world-leading work can be found at www.watoto.com.

About the Photographer

 Wes has been a professional photographer for 20 years and has traveled extensively with his firm, Skyepics (www.skyepics.com.au) capturing the lives of people and the places in which they live. Wes has presented at numerous exhibitions including "The Mystery of the Gobi" experience at the Palazzo Versace, where his photographs won national acclaim as he presented his journey as one of the first Western photographers through the remote, inaccessible Badanjilin Desert in China. Wes lives on the Gold Coast, Australia with his wife Jo and three children.

Wes's journey to build a classroom at a Watoto Child Care Village in Uganda changed his life. "As a professional photographer I have travelled around the world capturing through the lens, the lives of many different people in their own unique cultures. In all of this travel I have never experienced so much hope and inner joy than what my family and I observed while in Uganda, East Africa. Amidst the despair we came face to face with the hope, joy and thankfulness of the children of Watoto, and our lives have not been the same.

Kampala, the capital of Uganda is a city of immense contrasts from the outward displays of wealth and success for some, to the abject poverty for the vast majority. Within this struggle emerges Watoto Child Care Ministries as a beacon of hope for many who would otherwise be hopeless. Watoto picks up the parentless children, brings them into a loving family with a mother, brothers and sisters and a promise that they will never be abandoned again. The child's basic needs are cared for in a loving non-institutional setting, with first-rate medical attention, education and above all a faith and hope for the future. Watoto stands out where so many fail.

For me it has been a privilege and joy to capture these images, but my greatest hope is that you will catch hold of the vision of what is being done through Watoto." **Wes Palmer**

"Let the little children come to me, and do not hinder them, for the kingdom of God belongs to such as these." MARK 10:14

All Scripture references are from the New International Version.

Editor & Publisher - Stuart Robert (stuart@robert.com.au)

Principal Photographer - Wes Palmer (wes@skyepics.com.au)

Design - Silhouette Graphics, Southport, Gold Coast, Australia (contact@sgraphics.net)

The publisher is grateful for permission to be able to reproduce photos and text. While every effort has been made to trace copyright holders, the publisher would be pleased to hear from any not acknowledged here.

Special thanks to those incredible people that devote their lives to the Children of Watoto. Firstly to the founders and holders of the Watoto vision Gary and Marilyn Skinner. Your obedience to the God-given vision to found Watoto has led to the birth and development of one of the most unique and impactful organisations on earth. The Watoto story touches lives across the globe. Thank you for the decades of personal risk, sacrifice and commitment to the parentless children of Africa. Your story is nothing short of inspirational, it deserves to be told! To the Watoto staff in Uganda and around the world, your selfless love for the less fortunate is a beacon of light in a dark world. To Mark Bradshaw, the Managing Director of Watoto Australia, whose personal vision led to a Watoto office Down Under and Kim Caruso from Watoto USA for her words of encouragement and provision of photos and text.

Lastly to my beautiful wife, Chantelle, whose patience and support throughout my many projects is nothing short of uplifting. You are the greatest wife I could have prayed for, you will be the finest of mothers.

This journey of HOPE is dedicated to the children of Watoto. Your journey through the unbearable pain and suffering of losing one or both parents through to becoming Watoto children and the next generation of Uganda's and Africa's leaders is inspirational. You show day by day that it's not how your life begins, but how you live it through to the end that matters.

ISBN 0-9757567-0-2